Titus

Presented To

Granddaddy & Nana

From

May 10, 2009

Date

Copyright © 2008 by Christian Art Kids, an imprint of
Christian Art Publishers, PO Box 1599, Vereeniging, 1930, RSA

1025 N Lombard Road, PO Box 1443, Lombard, IL, 60148, USA

Developed in co-operation with Educational Publishing Concepts.

Copyright © 2007 by Carolyn Larsen
Illustrations © 2007 by Caron Turk
All rights reserved.

First edition 2008

Cover designed by Christian Art Kids

Set in 14 on 19 pt Palatino LT Std by Christian Art Kids

Printed in China

ISBN 978-1-86920-927-8

08 09 10 11 12 13 14 15 16 17 – 12 11 10 9 8 7 6 5 4 3

101 Bible Stories for Toddlers

Carolyn Larsen
Illustrated by Caron Turk

christian
art kids

Table of Contents

Dear Parents,

Once in a while someone will ask me whether I truly believe it is necessary to teach a toddler about the Bible. Each time my answer is a resounding YES. Of course it's true that a toddler's mind and heart cannot grasp the deep theological truths of the Bible yet, but he or she can certainly begin to learn of God's love and care for His creation. That knowledge is the groundwork for your child to learn to love and trust God with his or her own life.

As you read these Bible stories with your little one, my prayer is that the stories will stimulate conversation between you and your child. A toddler's questions can take you many places and provide opportunities for you to share simple stories of your own experience with God. I pray that God will use this simple book as a tool to draw your toddler into a relationship with Him.

Blessings,
Carolyn Larsen

A Brand New World

Genesis 1:1-2:3

God made everything!
He made the big, yellow sun
to shine in daytime. He made
the stars and moon for night.

God made kittens and puppies. He made birds.
He made fish, too. God made all animals.

God made flowers; red, yellow and pink.
He made trees and grass and bushes.
God made all plants.

14

God made big, big mountains.
He made deep, deep oceans.
God made the world and everything in it!

The Very First People

Genesis 2:4-25

God made the world.
He made oceans and mountains and animals and plants.
It was beautiful. But God was not finished.

God wanted someone to take care of the world.
He wanted someone to be His friend.

God took some dust from the ground. He made Adam, the first man. Adam would be God's friend.

God made Eve, the first woman.
She would be God's friend, too.
Now God was finished making things.
He was happy with all He had made.

A Beautiful Garden

Genesis 3

Adam and Eve lived in a beautiful garden. God made it just for them. It was called Eden.

The garden had everything Adam and Eve needed.
It had food. It had water.
They could go anywhere in the garden.

Adam and Eve had only one rule.
God said they should not eat the fruit
that grew on one certain tree.

Adam and Eve
ate that fruit.
God was sad.
He must
punish them.
They had to leave
the garden.
They could never
come back.

Noah Obeys

Genesis 6:1-7:10

Adam and Eve disobeyed God. That was called sin.
The people who lived after them sinned, too.
People did bad things.

God was sad. He did not like
what people were doing. Only one man
obeyed God. His name was Noah.

God told Noah to build a boat.
It would be a very big boat.
A flood was coming.
God wanted Noah to be safe.

Noah obeyed. He built the boat.
God sent animals to go in the boat.
Noah's family went inside the boat, too.

The Big, Big Flood

Genesis 7:11-9:19

Noah and his family were inside the boat.
The animals were in the boat, too.
Soon, it started to rain outside.

It rained and rained. It rained forty days and
forty nights. The big boat floated on the water.
Everyone inside the boat was safe.
Everything outside the boat flooded.

Finally the rain stopped.
Noah waited until all the water went away.
Noah and his family came out of the boat.
The animals came out of the boat.

God promised never to send a flood that big again.
He made a special sign as a reminder of His promise.
That sign is a rainbow!

The Tower of Babel

Genesis 11:1-9

One time some men started building a tower. They wanted it to be the tallest tower in the world.

The men were proud of
their big tower.
They felt important.
They felt so important that
they did not
think they needed
God anymore.

God was not happy with the men.
He made them stop building the tower.
He made them all speak in different languages.

Now they could not talk to one another.
Now they did not feel so important.
Now they needed God again.

Isaac Is Born

Genesis 21:1-7

God promised a son to Abraham and Sarah.
That made them happy.
They had wanted a baby for a long time.

They waited and waited.
But they still had no baby.
Now Abraham was 100 years old.
Sarah was 90 years old.

Were they too old to have a baby?
No, God always keeps His promises.
Sarah had a baby boy!
They named him Isaac.

Abraham and Sarah were very happy.
They thanked God for keeping His promises.
They thanked God for their son.

Jacob and Esau

Genesis 25:19-26

Isaac married Rebekah.
They were married a long time but had no children.
Isaac asked God to give them a child.

God answered Isaac's prayer.
Rebekah had two babies!
She had twin boys.
Isaac and Rebekah were very happy.

The first baby had red hair.
They named him Esau.
The second boy was Jacob.
He was holding his brother's heel when he was born.

When they grew up, Esau and Jacob
each led a group of people.
Esau's people served Jacob's people.

Esau Makes a Bad Choice

Genesis 25:27-34

When Esau grew up he was a hunter.
Jacob liked to stay at home and do things.

One day Esau came home from hunting.
He was hungry. "Jacob, give me some of that
stew you are cooking," he said.

"I will, if you give me your birthright," Jacob said.
The birthright belonged to the oldest son.
It meant he would lead the family someday.

Esau was very hungry.
He did not care about the birthright.
He gave away his birthright for a bowl of stew.

Peaceful Isaac

Genesis 26:12-25

Isaac was a farmer.
He owned lots of sheep and cattle.
He had many servants. Isaac was very rich.

Isaac needed water for his family and animals.
He dug wells to get water.
The Philistines did not like Isaac.
They filled his wells up with dirt.

Isaac moved. He dug more wells.
Some shepherds stole those wells.
Isaac would not fight them.
He dug new wells.

God was happy that Isaac did not fight.
He promised to give Isaac a big family.
He promised to bless Isaac.

Jacob's Trick

Genesis 27:1-40

Isaac was old. It was time to
give his blessing to his oldest son, Esau.
That meant Esau would be the family leader.

Isaac sent Esau out to hunt for food.
They would cook it and have dinner.
Then Isaac would give Esau the blessing.

While Esau was gone, Jacob dressed in Esau's clothes.
He made food and took it to his father.
He tricked Isaac.

Isaac did not know that it was Jacob.
He gave Jacob the blessing.
Now Jacob would lead the family instead of Esau.

Jacob Has a Dream

Genesis 28:10-22

Jacob stole his father's blessing from his brother.
Esau was very angry.
Jacob went away so he would be safe.

Jacob walked and walked.
He went a long way and got very tired.
So Jacob lay down and went to sleep.

While he was sleeping, Jacob had a dream.
He saw angels going up and down a ladder.
God was at the top of the ladder.

God said, "Jacob, I will take care of you."
Jacob said, "I will serve You, God."

Jacob and Rachel

Genesis 29:1-14

One day Jacob saw a beautiful woman.
She was taking care of her father's sheep.
Her name was Rachel.

Rachel had come to the well.
Her sheep needed water.
But a big stone covered the well.

Jacob moved the stone.
He helped Rachel get water for her sheep.
Rachel was glad that Jacob helped her.

Jacob knew he wanted to marry Rachel.
She wanted to marry him, too.

Jacob and Esau Meet

Genesis 32:1-21; 33:1-11

64

Jacob and his family were on a trip.
Jacob had many children.
He had many servants.
The traveling group was very big.

Then he heard that Esau was
coming down the road.
Esau had an army of 400 men
with him. Jacob was afraid.

Jacob prayed that God would protect him.
He prayed that Esau would not be angry anymore.
He even sent gifts to Esau.

Esau was not angry.
He wanted to be friends again, too.
Jacob was happy.

Joseph and His Brothers

Genesis 37:1-36

Jacob had twelve sons. Joseph was his favorite son. He gave Joseph special gifts.

Joseph's brothers were jealous of him.
Some of them wanted to kill him.
Then they met some men who were going to Egypt.

The men said they would buy Joseph.
They would take him to Egypt.
He would be a slave there.

Joseph's brothers sold him.
Now he would be a slave.
Jacob was sad.
He would miss Joseph.

Joseph Is Saved

Genesis 41:1-45

Poor Joseph. First his brothers sold him to be a slave.
Then he was put in jail but he had not done anything wrong.
Someone lied about him.

The king of Egypt had a dream.
He wanted to know what it meant.
But none of his wise men could explain it.

Joseph could explain the dream!
God helped him understand it.
The king was very happy.
He let Joseph out of jail.

The king knew Joseph was very wise.
He put Joseph in charge of all of Egypt.

Joseph Forgives

Genesis 45:1-15

Joseph's brothers came to Egypt.
They wanted to buy food.
They had to ask the ruler to sell them food.

The brothers did not know that the ruler was Joseph.
They thought Joseph was a slave somewhere.
But Joseph knew who they were.

Joseph could put his brothers in jail.
After all, they had been mean to him.
What would Joseph do?

Joseph forgave his brothers!
He brought them to Egypt to live with him.
Everyone was happy now!

Hebrew Slaves

Exodus 1

A long time after Joseph ruled Egypt
something bad happened. All the Hebrew
people were made slaves in Egypt.

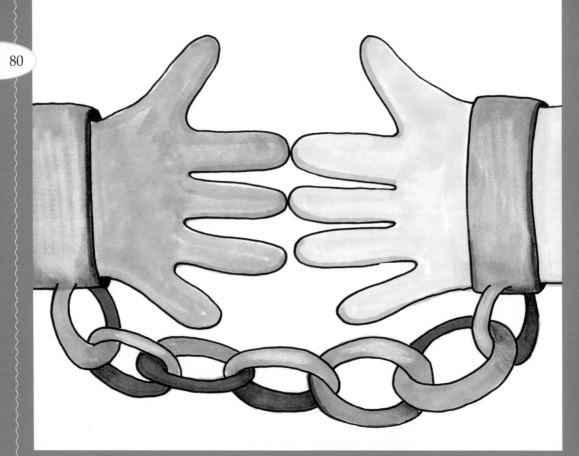

They had to work very hard.
They made bricks from mud and straw.
The king wanted more and more bricks.

God was good to the Hebrews.
He gave them many babies.
There were more and more Hebrews.

The king of Egypt did not want more Hebrews.
The king ordered his soldiers to hurt the Hebrew babies.

Moses Is Saved

Exodus 2:1-10

See that basket floating in the water?
See the little baby sleeping inside?
That is Baby Moses.

The soldiers were hurting Hebrew babies.
Moses' mother wanted him to be safe.
So, she hid Moses in the little basket boat.

A princess found the basket floating
on the water. She loved the little baby.
The princess took Moses to live with her in the palace.

Moses was safe now!
His mother was very happy.
Moses would grow up to be an Egyptian prince!

God Speaks to Moses

Exodus 3:1-4:17

The Hebrew people were still slaves in Egypt.
They asked God to help them.
God heard their prayers.

"Moses, help My people," a voice said. Moses looked to see who was speaking. All he saw was a bush that was on fire.

Flames burned in the bush.
But the bush did not burn up.
God's Spirit was in the bush.
God was speaking to Moses.

"Lead the people out of Egypt," God said.
He promised to help Moses.
"I will obey," Moses said.

God Helps Moses

Exodus 7-12

"God says to let the people leave Egypt," Moses said.
The king of Egypt said, "No!"
He did not want to lose his slaves.

Bad things began happening in Egypt.
God wanted the king to listen to Moses.
The king would not change his mind.

Moses asked again.
The king said, "No" again.
More bad things happened.
The king did not think
God was important.

After ten bad things happened,
the king said, "You can go."
Now he knew God was
the most powerful.

Leaving Egypt

Exodus 13:17-22

The Hebrew people were slaves in Egypt
for many, many years. God sent
Moses to lead them to freedom.

The people were excited to be free again.
Thousands and thousands of people
followed Moses out of Egypt.

Where would they go?
How would Moses know
where to lead the people?
God showed him!

A big tower of cloud led the
people in the daytime.
At night it became a tower of fire.
God's Spirit was leading the people!

The Red Sea

Exodus 14:5-31

Thousands of Hebrew slaves left Egypt.
The king of Egypt wanted them back.
He sent his army to get them.

The Red Sea was in front of the Hebrew people.
The army was coming behind them.
What would they do?
Were they trapped?

"Watch what God will do for you," Moses said.
The wind began to blow.
It blew so hard that it blew
the waters of the sea apart.

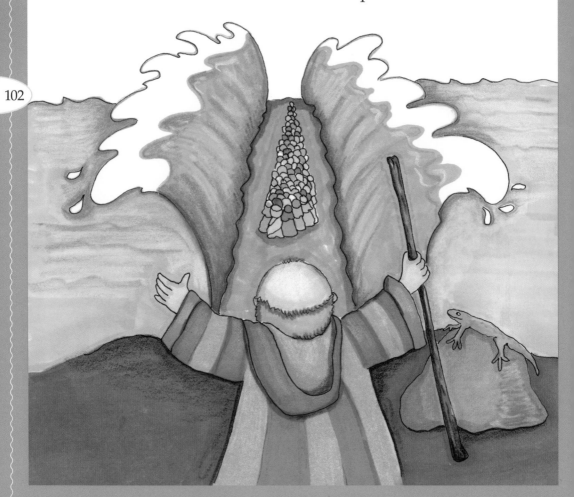

The people walked through the Red Sea on dry ground.
Then the waters went back to normal.
God saved them from the army!

Food for the People

Exodus 16

"We're hungry!" the people complained.
"We want food." Where would they get food?
What would they do?

Moses knew
what to do.
He asked God
to help them.
God took care
of the people!

Every morning food appeared on the ground.
It was called manna.
The people picked up all they needed.

Every day God sent birds for the people to catch.
Now they had all the food they needed.

Ten Important Rules

Exodus 20:1-21

"Moses, come up on the mountain," God said.
He wanted to talk to Moses.
Moses left the people and went up the mountain.

God told Moses the ways that the people should obey Him.
He wrote ten important rules on pieces of stone.

Moses took the stones down to the people.
"These are God's rules," he told the people.
"God wants you to obey them."

"We will obey," the people said.
When they obeyed they were happy.
But when they disobeyed they were not happy.

The Golden Calf

Exodus 32

Moses was up on the mountain talking to God.
He was gone a long time.
The people did not think he was coming back.

"We want a new god," the people said.
"We want a god we can see."
They used gold to make a statue of a calf.
It was their new god.

Moses heard the people singing.
He came down from the mountain
to see what they were doing.

Moses saw the golden calf.
He saw the people worshiping it.
He was angry with them.
"Follow God, not a statue!" he said.

Offerings for God

Exodus 35:4-9

"God wants us to build a house for Him," Moses told the people. "We must all give things to be used in it."

The people did give things for God's house.
Some brought gold, silver and bronze.

Others brought beautiful colored
cloth and fine spices and oils.

The people brought many gifts for God's house.
Finally, Moses said, "Stop!
We have all we need to build God's house."

God's House in the Desert

Exodus 35:10-40:38

The people worked together.
They built a beautiful tent to be God's house.
It was called a tabernacle.

God told Moses how to build the tabernacle.
He told Moses what to put inside it.
It was filled with beautiful things.

The tent-house could be packed up
and moved when the people moved.
It was a wonderful place to worship God.

God was happy with the tabernacle.
He met with Moses there.
He told Moses things to tell the people.

The Twelve Spies

Numbers 13

"That land up ahead is going to
be your land," God said.
That made the people happy.
They had been walking in the
desert for a long time.

The Hebrews sent twelve spies in
to see what the land was like.
They checked to see what the
people were like.

Ten of the spies said, "The people are giants.
We can't win a battle against them!
We don't stand a chance."

Two spies said, "We can win. God will help."
But the people listened to the ten spies.
They did not trust God to help them.

The Battle of Jericho

Joshua 6

The Hebrews stood outside of Jericho.
They had to capture this city to get into
the land God promised them.

But there were big walls around Jericho.
How could they get inside?
"Do what I tell you," God told Joshua.

"March around Jericho once a day," God said.
"Just march, nothing else."
That's what the people did.

On the seventh day when they
marched the big walls fell down!
Joshua led the people in to capture the city!

The Three Hundred Soldiers

Judges 7

Gideon's army was going to fight the Midianites.
His army had many soldiers.
"You have too many soldiers," God said.

Gideon sent some soldiers home.
"Your army is still too big," God said.
More soldiers were sent away.
Only 300 soldiers were left.

If they won now it would be because of
God's help. God told Gideon what to do.
Each soldier lit a torch and
covered it with a jar.

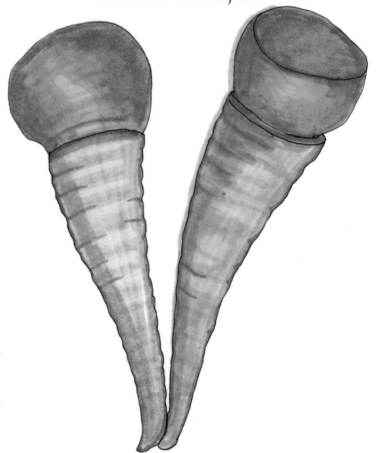

Gideon gave a sign and they broke the jars,
shouted, and ran into the enemy camp.
The Midianites got scared and ran away.
Gideon's little army won!

Samson and the Lion

Judges 14

Samson was the strongest
man in the world. He
was strong because
he obeyed God.

One day Samson was walking down the road.
Suddenly a lion jumped out at him.

What would Samson do?
He had fought men.
He had fought whole armies.
But was he strong enough to fight a lion?

Yes, he was! Samson grabbed the lion.
He fought the lion with his bare hands.
Samson won! God helped Samson win.

Loyal Ruth

The Book of Ruth

Ruth and Naomi were sad because their husbands had died.
Naomi wanted to go home to Israel.

"I will go with you," Ruth said. Naomi thought
Ruth should stay with her own family.
But Ruth wanted to help Naomi.

Naomi was too old to work.
Ruth had to find a way to get
food for them in Israel.

Ruth worked in the fields to get food.
She picked up grain the workers had dropped.
Ruth loved Naomi.
She took good care of her.

God Speaks to Samuel

1 Samuel 3:1-18

Samuel was a little boy.
He lived in the temple.
He worked there and
helped the priest.

One night Samuel was very tired.
He went to bed.
He was sleeping when
a voice woke him up.

Three times the voice
called Samuel.
It was God! God was
speaking to Samuel.

146

God told Samuel some important things.
Samuel listened carefully.
It is important to listen to God, isn't it?

A King for Israel

1 Samuel 10:17-27

"We want a king like other nations," the people said.
God did not want them to have a king.

Samuel told them that God should be
their only ruler. The people said,
"No, we want a king."

God listened to the people.
He chose a man to be king.
He sent Samuel to tell the
people which man would be king.

Samuel called the people together.
"God chose Saul to be your king," he said.
Saul was taller than any other man.

David and Goliath

1 Samuel 17

David was a young boy.
He was not a soldier.
Goliath was a soldier.
He was a giant soldier – 9 feet tall!

Goliath said bad things about God. He made fun of God's army. He called for someone to fight him.

David was the only one brave enough to fight him.
But he just had a sling and some stones to fight with.
How could he win?

David asked God to help him.
God did help the young boy defeat the giant soldier!

Best Friends

1 Samuel 18:1-4

After David killed the
giant, he was famous
and important.
King Saul invited him to
live in the palace.

King Saul's son lived in the palace, too.

His name was Jonathan.

He was a prince.

Prince Jonathan knew that David killed the giant.
He knew that God was with David.
Prince Jonathan and David became best friends.

They promised to be friends forever.
Jonathan gave David special gifts to
show how much he loved him.

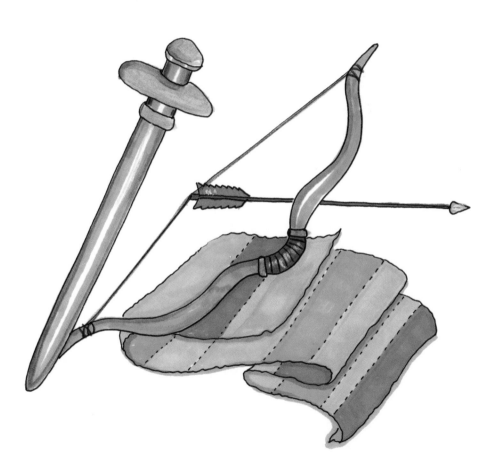

David and Mephibosheth

2 Samuel 9

King Saul died in a battle and David became king.
King David remembered his promise to always
be friends with Jonathan.

Jonathan was killed in battle, too.
David was sad. He would miss his friend.
He wanted to show kindness to Jonathan's family.

David searched for his friend's family.
He found Jonathan's son named Mephibosheth.
His legs had been hurt.
He was crippled.

David brought Mephibosheth
to the palace to live with him.
He gave him gifts and took care
of Mephibosheth and his family.

King Solomon's Dream

1 Kings 3:1-15; 2 Chronicles 1:1-13

One night King Solomon was sleeping.
God spoke to him in a dream.
"I will give you whatever you
ask for," God said.

King Solomon wanted to be a good leader.
He said, "Help me to be wise.
Help me to do a good job leading my people."

God was happy with the king's request.
He was pleased that Solomon didn't
ask for money or fame.

"I will give you wisdom," God said.
"I will also give you riches and make you famous."

God's Special House

1 Kings 5-7; 2 Chronicles 2:1-5:1

King Solomon decided to build a special temple.
It would be God's house.
The people could worship Him there.

King Solomon got thousands and
thousands of workers.
Kings from other countries sent special
wood and stone and other supplies.

It took a long time to build the temple.
It was decorated inside with gold and jewels.
It was beautiful.

"The temple is finished," Solomon declared.
"Come and worship God in His house!"
The people did come!
They worshiped God in the temple.

Food for Elijah

1 Kings 17:1-6

No rain fell on the land for a few years.
The ground dried up.
No food could grow without water.

The people needed food.
Elijah needed food, too.
He was God's servant.
He was doing God's work.

God sent black birds called ravens to Elijah.
The birds brought food to him each
morning and again each night.

God took care of Elijah.
"Thank You, God," Elijah said every day.

Bread for Elijah

1 Kings 17:8-16

God sent Elijah to a certain town.
He said, "There is a woman there
who will give you food."

When Elijah saw the woman he asked for some bread.
"I have none," the woman said.
"I have only a little flour and oil.
After I make one last loaf of bread, my son and I will die."

"Don't worry," Elijah said.
"Make bread and share it with me.
God will take care of you."
So the woman did.

God gave her more and more flour and oil.
The woman always had enough food.
God took care of her.
God took care of Elijah, too!

The Real God

1 Kings 18:19-39

Some people did not believe in God.
They believed in a fake god named Baal.
Elijah knew that God was the real God.

"Let's have a contest," Elijah said.
"We'll see if Baal has any power or not."
Four hundred and fifty followers of
Baal came to the contest.

They called for Baal to send fire to burn up some meat.
Of course, Baal could not do it.
"It's God's turn now," Elijah said.

"Send fire," Elijah prayed.
God sent fire that burned up the meat,
the stones and even the water around it.
Everyone knew that God was the real God.

Elisha's New Room

2 Kings 4:8-17

Elisha was God's servant.
He traveled from town to town.
He taught people about God.

In one town a woman said,
"Have dinner with my husband and me."
Any time Elisha was in their town he ate with them.

Then the woman had an idea.
"Let's make a room for Elisha to stay in," she said.
They made a room just for Elisha.

When Elisha visited their town he had a place to stay.
Elisha was very thankful for their kindness.

Money for God's House

2 Kings 12:1-16; 2 Chronicles 24:1-14

God's house was in bad shape. Repairs were needed.
But no one was taking care of it.
"It's time to fix God's house," King Joash said.

He put a large chest by the altar.
The chest had a hole cut in the top.
The people who came to worship put their
offerings in the chest.

When the chest was full it was emptied
so more money could be put in.
Lots of money was collected.

After a while there was enough
money to repair God's house.
Workers were hired and God's
house was beautiful again.

The Walls of Jerusalem

Nehemiah 2:1-7:3

Nehemiah was sad.
He was sad because the big walls around
the city of Jerusalem were falling down.
Someone needed to repair them.

The walls kept the city safe.
The walls kept the enemies out.
Nehemiah wanted Jerusalem to be safe.

Nehemiah decided he would fix the walls.
He asked some people to help him.
They said they would help.

Other men tried to stop Nehemiah from fixing the walls.
But Nehemiah worked even harder.
Soon the walls were big and strong again!

Beautiful Queen Esther

The Book of Esther

Esther was the most beautiful girl in the land.
The king chose her to be his wife.
Now she was Queen Esther.

One of the king's servants did not like the Jewish people.
Haman wanted to hurt them.
He did not know that Queen Esther was Jewish.

The king did not know his wife was Jewish, either.
Queen Esther told the king about Haman's plan.
She asked him to stop Haman.

The king loved Queen Esther very much.
He stopped Haman and he punished him.
Queen Esther was very brave.

Job

The Book of Job

Job was a rich man. He had a big family.
He owned many animals. Job loved God very much.

One day bad things started happening to Job. His children died. He got sores all over his body. His animals died.

Job's friends thought God was punishing him.
They thought he should get angry at God.
But Job knew that God still loved him.
He would not get angry.

God was very happy with Job.
He gave him more children.
He gave him more riches than he had before.
God loved Job very much.

Daniel Eats Right

Daniel 1

Daniel and his friends were captured by
soldiers from another country.
They would be taught how to serve the
king of the new land.

"The king has ordered special food for you,"
the guard told Daniel.
"It will make you strong and healthy."
The food had been offered to the king's gods.
Daniel did not want to eat it.

"Please, just let us eat vegetables and drink water.
I promise that we will be stronger than
everyone else," Daniel said.

The guard let them try it for a few days.
Sure enough, God made Daniel and his friends
stronger and healthier than all the other boys!

Daniel and the Lions

Daniel 6

Daniel sat next to his window and prayed to God every day.
Daniel loved God very much.

Some men did not like Daniel. They wanted to get him into trouble. The men tricked the king. They had him make a law that people could not pray to God.

Daniel kept right on praying.
He was arrested and put in with hungry lions.
The king was sad. He liked Daniel.
"I hope your God protects you," the king said.

God did! He kept the lions' mouths closed all night.
The next morning Daniel was just fine.
God loved Daniel very much.

Jonah Disobeys

The Book of Jonah

"Jonah," God said, "Go to Nineveh.
Teach the people there to obey Me."
Jonah did not want to go.
He did not like the people in Nineveh.

Jonah ran the other way.
He got on a boat going far away from Nineveh.
God knew where Jonah was.
He sent a big storm on the sea.

The sailors were scared.
They threw Jonah into the water.
God sent a big fish to swallow Jonah right up.

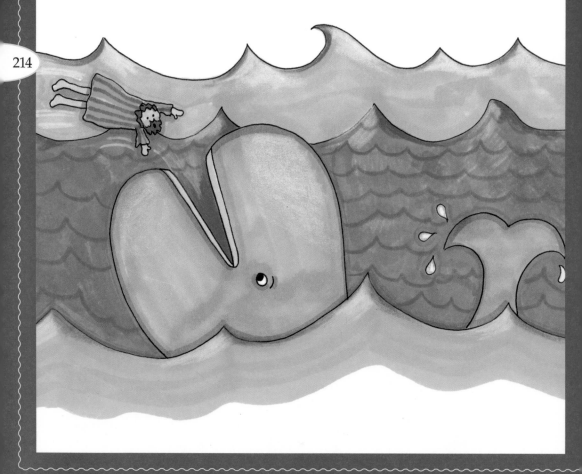

Jonah decided he would obey God now.
God told the fish to spit him out.
Jonah went right to Nineveh.
He taught the people to obey God.

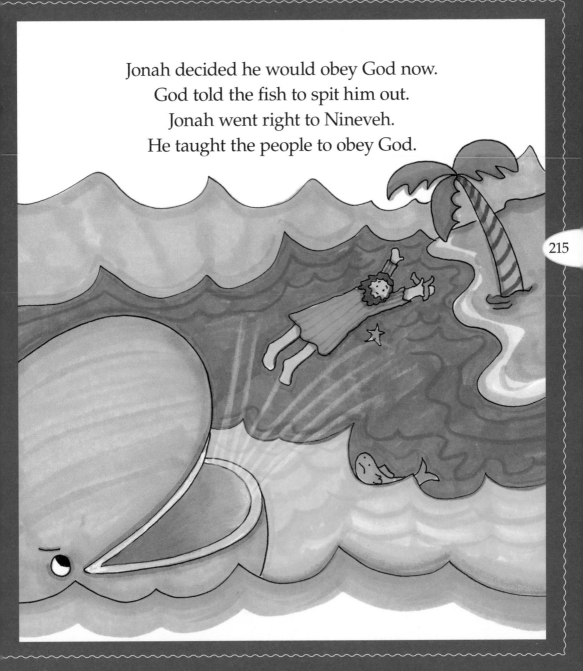

An Angel Talks to Mary

Luke 1:26-38

Something special happened to a
young girl named Mary.
She lived in Nazareth.
Mary loved God very much.

One day an angel came to see Mary. That was a surprise! The angel had exciting news for Mary.

"You are going to have a baby," the angel said.
"He will be God's Son.
God says to name Him Jesus."

Mary was glad to do
what God wanted.
She was happy to obey Him.

Baby Jesus Is Born

Luke 2:1-7

Mary and Joseph had to go to Bethlehem.
They traveled a long way.
Mary was tired.
It was time for her baby to be born.

220

Mary and Joseph could not find any place to stay in Bethlehem. They had to go into a stable to sleep by the animals.

Baby Jesus was born that night.
Mary wrapped Him in cloth.
She laid Baby Jesus down to sleep in a feedbox.

Be quiet chickens!
Be quiet sheep!
Don't wake up Baby Jesus!

Shepherds Visit Jesus

Luke 2:8-20

Some shepherds were in a field
outside of Bethlehem.
Some were watching the sheep.
Some were sleeping.

Suddenly the sky was very bright.
It was an angel! The angel said, "God's
Son was born tonight in Bethlehem.
He is your Savior!"

Then the sky was filled with many angels.
They were all singing, "Praise God! Hallelujah!"

The shepherds rushed into town.
They wanted to see the Baby.
They found Jesus in the stable,
just as the angel said they would.

Wise Men Visit Jesus

Matthew 2:1-12

"Look, there is a special star in
the sky," a wise man said.
He knew what it meant –
a special king had been born.

228

The wise men packed wonderful gifts.
They got on their camels and followed the star.
It moved across the sky. The wise men
followed it for a long time.

The star led them all the way to Bethlehem.
It led them right to the house where Jesus
lived with Mary and Joseph.

The wise men were very happy to see Jesus.
They gave Him gifts of gold,
frankincense and myrrh.

Safety in Egypt

Matthew 2:13-18

"Wake up, Joseph!" an angel said.
"You must leave Bethlehem right now!
The king wants to hurt Baby Jesus."

Joseph woke up Mary.
They left for Egypt in the middle of the night.
That's where the angel told Joseph to go.

The bad king sent soldiers to Bethlehem.
They looked everywhere for Jesus.
But they could not find Him.

Joseph, Mary and Jesus lived in
Egypt until the bad king died.
Jesus was safe there.
God took care of them.

The First Time Jesus Taught

Luke 2:41-52

Mary and Joseph went to Jerusalem
each year to celebrate Passover.
That was an important religious holiday.

The year that Jesus was twelve years old
something unusual happened.
Mary and Joseph started home after the holiday.
But Jesus was not with them.
They could not find Him anywhere!

They hurried back to Jerusalem.
They looked everywhere they could think of.
Finally they found Jesus.
He was in the temple.

Jesus was talking to the teachers there.
He was teaching them about God!
The teachers were surprised that
He knew so much about God.

John the Baptist

Matthew 3:1-12; Mark 1:1-8; Luke 3:1-18

A man named John had a special job.
He told people that Jesus was coming.
He did not have a temple or a church to teach in.

John taught outside.
He taught beside rivers.
He taught on mountains.
People came to hear him.

John did not look like a teacher.
He wore clothes made from camel skins.
He ate locusts for dinner.

John didn't care how he looked or what he ate.
He just wanted all the people to be
ready to meet Jesus.

Jesus Is Baptized

Matthew 3:13-17; Mark 1:9-11; Luke 3:21, 22; John 1:31-34

People listened to John teach about Jesus. When people said they wanted to obey God John baptized them in the river.

One day Jesus Himself came to John.
"Baptize Me, too," Jesus said.
"I want to obey God."

John said, "I can't baptize You.
You are the one I'm teaching about."
But Jesus wanted John to baptize Him.

So John baptized Jesus in the river.
God was very happy when Jesus was baptized.
He said, "This is My Son.
He pleases Me very much!"

The Temptation of Jesus

Matthew 4:1-11; Mark 1:12, 13; Luke 4:1-13

Jesus was ready to start teaching about God. Satan did not want Him to do that. Satan wanted Jesus to obey him.

Satan took Jesus into the desert.
Jesus was all by Himself for 40 days.
He did not have any food for all that time.

Jesus was tired and hungry.
Satan came to Him and said,
"I will give You wonderful things.
But You must obey me instead of God."

Jesus would not listen to Satan.
"I must obey only God," He said.
"Nothing is more important than that."

Jesus Teaches Nicodemus

John 3:1-21

A man named Nicodemus came to see Jesus.
Nicodemus was a religious teacher.
He knew a lot about God.

"How can I know God better?" Nicodemus asked Jesus.
He had heard Jesus teaching. He knew that
Jesus knew more about God than he did.

"Listen to Me," Jesus said.
"Knowing God is like being born a second time.
Knowing God gives you a brand new life."

"I want that new life," Nicodemus said.
He was very glad he came to talk to Jesus.

Peter Follows Jesus

Luke 5:1-11

Peter had fished all night but he did not catch any fish.
He was on shore cleaning his fishing nets.

Jesus was nearby.
He was teaching some people.
They were crowding around Him.
Jesus climbed into Peter's boat.
He asked Peter to push it out into
the water a little bit.

Jesus finished teaching.
He told Peter to throw the nets out again.
Peter did not want to. He had fished
all night without catching any fish.

When Peter threw the net out it filled up with fish.
He had so many fish he couldn't pull the net back in!
He left his boat right there and followed Jesus!

A Tax Collector Follows Jesus

Matthew 9:9-13; Mark 2:14-17; Luke 5:27-32

People did not like tax collectors.
The tax collectors often cheated the people.
They took money from the people for themselves.

Matthew was a tax collector.
When Jesus saw Matthew, He said, "Follow Me."
Matthew got right up and followed Jesus.

Matthew had a dinner at his house.
His tax collector friends came.
Jesus came, too. Some people thought Jesus
should not eat with them.

Jesus came to teach people about God.
He believed that the tax collectors needed
to know about God, too.

Twelve Special Helpers

Mark 3:13-19; Luke 6:12-16

Many people followed Jesus.
Many people listened to Him teach.
Many believed in God.
A crowd of people followed Jesus wherever He went.

One day Jesus said, "I am going to
choose some special helpers.
These helpers will be My closest friends."

Jesus chose twelve men.
They were called His disciples.
They stayed with Jesus all the time.

Jesus taught these men many things about obeying God.
Jesus gave these men special jobs to do for Him.

Jesus at the Well

John 4:1-42

Jesus had been walking for a long time.
He was hot and thirsty. He saw
a woman getting water from a well.
"Please give Me a drink of water," He said.

"Why are You talking to me?" the woman asked.
"Jewish people do not talk to my people."

"Listen to Me and I will give you something better than water," Jesus said.
He was talking about knowing God.

"I will understand about God when God's
Son comes," the woman answered.
"I am God's Son," Jesus said.
Now the woman was very glad she talked to Jesus!

Through the Roof

Matthew 9:1-8; Mark 2:1-12; Luke 5:17-26

Jesus was teaching a crowd of people.
So many people had come to listen that no
one else could get inside the house.

272

Four friends wanted Jesus to help their friend. He could not walk. They knew Jesus could heal him. But they couldn't get him through the crowd.

How would they get their friend into the room?
They went up on the roof.
They dug a hole and lowered their friend
through the roof to Jesus.

Jesus saw how much faith they had.
He saw that they believed He could heal their friend.
So, He did! "Thank You," said the friends.
"Thank You," said the healed man.

The Sermon on the Mount

Matthew 5-7

People followed Jesus everywhere He went. Crowds gathered to hear Him teach about living for God and how to treat each other.

One day a crowd of people followed
Jesus to a mountain.
Jesus stood on the side of the
mountain and taught the people.
The people sat on the ground below Him.

"Live for God," Jesus taught.
"Obey Him. Be kind to other people.
Treat others the way you want them to treat you."

The people listened carefully.
They wanted to learn how to live
the way God wanted them to live.

A Sad Mother

Luke 7:11-17

One day Jesus saw a sad woman.
She was crying and crying.
She was sad because her son died.

"Don't be sad," Jesus said to the mother.
He was sad because she felt so bad.

Jesus walked over to the dead boy.
"Get up," He said. The people around Him were confused.
Did Jesus think a dead boy would stand up?

But the boy did get up! He wasn't dead
anymore. Jesus brought him back to life.
The mother had her son back.
"Thank You," she said to Jesus.

A Man of Great Faith

Matthew 8:5-13; Luke 7:1-10

An important man came to see Jesus.
He was a soldier.
He was in charge of many other soldiers.

284

"Please help my servant,"
the important man begged Jesus.
"He is at home. He is in terrible pain.
He can't walk."

"I will come to your house," Jesus said.
But the important man stopped Jesus.
"You only need to speak the words and he
will be well," the man said.

"You have amazing faith in Me," Jesus said.
"Your servant is already better." Sure enough,
the sick man was healed at that very moment.

Jesus Teaches with Stories

Matthew 13:1-9; Mark 4:1-9; Luke 8:4-8

Jesus had important lessons to teach.
He knew that sometimes the best way
to explain a lesson was by telling a story.

One time Jesus sat in a boat on a lake and taught.
The people crowded around the edge of the lake to listen.

Jesus' story that day was about seeds.
Some seed fell on bad ground and didn't grow.
Some seed was gobbled up by birds before it could grow.

Some seed grew into plants but weeds choked it out. Some seed took root and grew into good plants. Jesus was teaching a lesson about people who let God's love grow deep in their hearts.

A Bad Storm

Matthew 8:23-27; Mark 4:36-41; Luke 8:22-25

Jesus and His disciples got into a boat.
They planned to sail across the lake.
Jesus went to the back of the boat and fell asleep.

292

Suddenly a terrible storm came up.
Strong winds blew rain into the disciples' faces.
The waves bounced the little boat up and down.

The disciples were afraid the boat was going to sink.
Jesus was still asleep.
"Wake up!" the disciples said. "Help us.
We're going to drown."

Jesus looked at the storm and said,
"Be still!" The storm stopped right away.
Jesus was sad that His disciples didn't
trust Him to keep them safe.

Jesus Helps a Little Girl

Matthew 9:18-26; Mark 5:22-43; Luke 8:41-56

Jairus loved his little girl very much.
When she got sick, he went to Jesus for help.
"Please come to my house. My daughter is very sick."

But a servant came up to Jairus and said,
"Your little girl has died."
Jairus was very sad.
He turned to go home.

"Wait," Jesus said.
He went home with Jairus.
"Your daughter is not dead.
She is just sleeping," He said.

Jesus sent everyone out of her room.
Then He said, "Get up, little girl."
She did! The little girl was alive again!

A Really Big Picnic

Matthew 14:13-21; Mark 6:32-44; Luke 9:10-17; John 6:1-13

One time 5,000 people came to hear Jesus teach.
Mothers, fathers and children sat on the ground
and listened to Him for a long time.

Pretty soon the people were hungry.
"Get food for them," Jesus said.
But the disciples didn't have any food.

"You can have my lunch," a boy said.
He had five small loaves of bread and two fish.
Jesus took the boy's lunch.
He thanked God for it.

Jesus broke the bread and fish into pieces.
His disciples passed it out to the people.
All 5,000 had enough to eat.
In fact, there were leftovers!

Walking on Water

Matthew 14:22-33; Mark 6:45-51; John 6:15-21

Jesus' disciples were in a boat.
They were crossing a big lake.
Jesus had stayed behind to pray.

A big storm blew up on the lake.
The disciples' boat was filling up with water.
The disciples thought they were going to die.

Jesus knew His friends were in trouble.
He went to help them.
He walked on top of the water to get to them.

"Stop blowing wind! Stop rain!" Jesus said.
The wind and rain stopped right away.
Even the wind and rain listened to Jesus.

The Good Samaritan

Luke 10:25-37

Jesus told this story:
A Jewish man was grabbed by robbers.
They beat him and left him to die.

The poor man needed help.
A church leader came down the road.
But he didn't help the hurt man.

A man who worked in a church came by next.
He didn't help either.
He crossed the road to get away
from the hurt man.

Next, a man from Samaria came by.
He stopped and helped the hurt man.
"This is the way you should treat
others," Jesus said.

Jesus Visits Mary and Martha

Luke 10:38-42

Jesus came to visit two sisters
named Mary and Martha.
They were good friends of His.
They were happy to see Him.

Martha went right to the kitchen.
She started making dinner for
Jesus and His friends.

Mary sat down next to Jesus and
listened to His teaching.
She loved learning about God.

"Make Mary help me," Martha complained to Jesus.
But Jesus told Martha to stop cooking.
He said it was more important to learn about God.

Finding a Lost Sheep

Matthew 18:10-14, Luke 15:1-7

A shepherd had 100 sheep.
He protected them from wild animals.
He made sure they had food and water.

One day one of his sheep got lost.
The shepherd could not find it anywhere.

He left the other 99 sheep alone
while he looked for the lost sheep.
He was very happy when he found it.

That's how much Jesus loves you!
He will help you find God.
He will be so happy when you do!

The Lost Son

Luke 15:11-32

This boy is sad. He is lonely.
He misses his family.
Here's what happened . . .

"Give me money," the boy told his father.
He moved to a big city and spent all the money.
Now he has to take care of pigs to get food.

"I miss my father. I want to go home," the boy said.
But would his father forgive him?

Yes, he would! His father was so happy to have his son back.
He threw a big party! It was a grand celebration.
God forgives us, too, each time we ask Him.

Lazarus, Come Forth!

John 11:1-44

Lazarus was very sick.
His sisters, Mary and Martha, sent for Jesus.
They knew He could help.

But before Jesus came, Lazarus died.
Mary and Martha were very sad.
Jesus was very sad, too.

Jesus went to the tomb where Lazarus was buried.
What was He going to do?

"Lazarus, come forth!" Jesus called.
Lazarus walked out of the tomb.
He was alive again! Jesus has power
over everything – even death!

Ten Sick Men

Luke 17:11-19

Jesus was walking along a road when some men stopped Him. All of them were sick with a very bad illness.

The disease they had was so bad that they could not be around other people. They could not live with their families. They could not hug their children or even play with them.

"Help us," they asked Jesus.
Of course, He did.
Jesus healed all of them.
They were each completely well.

Nine of the men ran off right away.
Only one man said, "Thank You, Jesus."
We should always remember to thank
Jesus for all He does for us.

Jesus Loves the Little Children

Matthew 19:13-15; Mark 10:13-16; Luke 18:15-17

People loved Jesus.
Moms and dads brought their children to Jesus.
They wanted Him to bless their little ones.

The disciples said, "No, Jesus does not have time for babies." But they were wrong.

"Bring the children to Me," Jesus said.
He loved the little children.
The little children loved Him, too.

Jesus said that everyone should trust God the way children do. Jesus blessed every little child that was brought to Him.

A Blind Man Sees

Matthew 20:29-34; Mark 10:46-52; Luke 18:35-43

"Jesus, help me," a blind man called out.
The people beside him on the road told him to be quiet.
They did not think he should bother Jesus.

Jesus stopped walking. He called the man to come to Him. "Go on," the crowd said. "Jesus wants you to come."

"What do you want Me to do for you?" Jesus asked the man.
"I would like to see," the man answered.

"Since you believe in Me so much, you will see," Jesus said. Right away, the man could see again! "Thank You, thank You," the man said!

Little Zacchaeus

Luke 19:1-10

Zacchaeus was a tax collector. He cheated people.
He took more money than they owed.
The people did not like Zacchaeus.

One day Zacchaeus heard that Jesus was coming. He wanted to see Him. But the road was crowded with people who wanted to see Jesus.

Zacchaeus was too short to see over the crowd.
No one would let him in.
Zacchaeus had an idea.
He climbed a tree so he could see.

Jesus saw Zacchaeus in the tree.
"Come down," He said. "I want to talk to you."
Zacchaeus was happy to come down.
He was happy to talk to Jesus.

The Triumphal Entry

Matthew 21:1-11; Mark 11:1-10; Luke 19:28-38; John 12:12-15

Jesus sent two of His disciples into Jerusalem.
He told them where to find a donkey.
They should ask the owner if they could borrow it.

The disciples found the donkey and brought it to Jesus.
Jesus rode into Jerusalem on the donkey.

People crowded around Him on the street.
"Praise God," the people shouted.
"Here comes our king!"

The people were excited about Jesus coming.
They spread their coats on the ground
for the donkey to walk on.
They waved palm branches. They cheered.

A Generous Gift

Mark 12:41-44; Luke 21:1-4

The temple was filled with people.
They came to give their offerings.
Jesus and His friends were there, too.

The rich men put lots of money in the offering.
They were proud that they gave so
much money to God.

One woman came to give an offering, too.
She was a poor widow.
She gave only two small coins.

Jesus saw what she gave.
"Look," He said to His friends.
"That woman gave more than all the others.
They gave their extra money.
But she gave all she had."

The Last Supper

Matthew 26:17-30; Mark 14:12-26; Luke 22:7-23; John 13:1-30

Jesus and His disciples ate a special supper together.
It was the last supper He had with His friends.

Jesus broke bread into pieces.
He passed it out to His friends.
He served wine to them, too.

Jesus told His friends that He would die soon.
They didn't understand what He was talking about.

"Remember Me," Jesus said.
When churches serve communion,
they are remembering Jesus' death.

Praying in a Garden

Matthew 26:36-46; Mark 14:32-42; Luke 22:40-46

"Come with Me," Jesus said.
He took three of His closest friends to a garden.

"Wait here and pray," He told them.
Jesus went on a little farther.
He knelt down and prayed for God's will to be done.

While Jesus was praying some
soldiers came and arrested Him.

Jesus wanted to do God's will even
if that meant doing something hard.

Jesus Dies

Matthew 27:32-56; Mark 15:21-41; Luke 23:26-49; John 19:16-30

The soldiers nailed Jesus to a cross.
He had not done anything wrong.
There was no reason for them to kill Him.

Jesus did not fight against the soldiers.
He let them kill Him because He loved people.
He came to earth to do this for us.

God does not allow sin or bad things in heaven.
But Jesus died for our sins.
He took our sins away.

Because we believe that Jesus died for our sins,
we can go to heaven someday. "Thank You,
Jesus, for loving us so much!"

The Women at the Tomb

Matthew 28:1-10; Mark 16:1-8; Luke 24:1-12

Jesus' friends were very sad when He died.
They did not understand why anyone would hurt Him.

A couple of days after He died, some women
went to where He was buried. They wanted
to put perfume and oils on Jesus' body.
That was their custom.

But when they got to the tomb, they had a surprise!
Jesus was gone! An angel said, "Jesus is not here.
He is alive again!"

The women were so excited.
They ran all the way to town to tell Jesus' other friends.
That is exactly what the angel told them to do!

Returning to Heaven

Mark 16:19-20; Luke 24:50-53; Acts 1:9-11

After Jesus came back to life, He came to see His friends.
They were very happy to see Him!

Jesus and His friends went to a place outside of town.
"I am going away now," Jesus told His friends.

"But I'm sending the Holy Spirit to you," He said.
While Jesus was speaking, His body floated up into the sky.

As His friends watched, Jesus disappeared.
Suddenly two angels came.
"Stop looking for Jesus," they said.
"He has gone back to heaven."

The Holy Spirit

Acts 2:1-13

Jesus' followers met together in a room.
They talked about Him.
They talked about serving God.

Suddenly there was a noise that sounded like the wind.
A little flame appeared above every person.

No one was afraid.
They knew that this meant the Holy Spirit had come.
Jesus had promised to send the Holy Spirit to them.

The Holy Spirit would give them power and energy to tell other people about Jesus!

Peter Heals a Crippled Man

Acts 3:1-10

Peter and John were on their way to the temple.
They went every day for prayer time.

A man called to them, "Will you give me some money?"
The man had been crippled his whole life.

Every day someone carried him to a place by the temple gate. He begged from people who were going in to pray.

"I have something better than money," Peter said.
"In Jesus' name I tell you to get up and walk!"
The man did! His legs were healed!

Philip and the Ethiopian

Acts 8:26-40

"Follow that chariot," an angel told Philip.
The man in the chariot was important.
He lived in Ethiopia.

The man was reading verses about Jesus from the Bible.
"Do you understand what you are reading?" Philip asked.
"No," the man said.

So Philip told him about Jesus.
He told him that Jesus died for his sins.
The man accepted Jesus as his Savior!

He wanted to be baptized right away.
So Philip baptized the man.
He was very glad that Philip obeyed the angel!

Saul Follows Jesus!

Acts 9:1-9

Saul was mean! He did not want anyone to follow Jesus.
When he found people who did, he put them in jail!

One day Saul was traveling to a new
city where he could arrest Christians.
A bright light shone down on him.
It was so bright that he couldn't see!

"Stop hurting Me and start working for Me," a voice said. It was Jesus! Now Saul knew that Jesus was real.

From that moment on Saul lived for Jesus.
He taught many, many others to follow Jesus, too.

Saul's Friends Help Him

Acts 9:20-25

Saul wanted everyone to know Jesus.
Saul's old friends were not happy about that.
They still did not like Christians.

They wanted to stop Saul from preaching.
They met together to come up with a plan.
Saul's old friends decided to kill him.

Saul heard about the plan.
He knew they were watching for him.
But, how could Saul get safely out of town?

The Christians helped him.
They put Saul in a basket and lowered him over the city walls.
The bad men did not even know he was gone!

Barnabas

Acts 9:26-31

Saul used to hate Christians.
But he loved Jesus now.
He wanted to do God's work.
He made a new start.

But when he came to Jerusalem the Christians
were not so sure they should trust Saul.
They were still afraid of him.

Barnabas stepped in.
He told everyone that Saul trusted Jesus now.
They did not need to be afraid of him anymore.

Then the Christians welcomed Saul.
He spent the rest of his life teaching about God.
He wrote many books that are in the Bible.

A Good Friend Named Dorcas

Acts 9:36-43

Dorcas was a good friend.
She helped many people.
Her friends loved her very much.

Dorcas liked to make clothes.
She made robes and clothes for her friends.
She helped people who were poor.

When Dorcas got sick and died, her friends
were very sad. They thought Peter could
help so they sent for him.

"Dorcas," Peter said, "Get up."
Dorcas did! God made her alive again.
"Thank You, God," her friends said.

Peter Escapes from Jail

Acts 12:1-17

Peter was in jail. He was chained to two guards.
Soldiers were all around him.

Peter's friends were praying for him.
They prayed together asking
God to keep him safe.

Peter was sleeping when he heard a
voice say, "Get up!" It was an angel!
Peter's chains fell off and he got up.

The angel walked him right past the
guards and out of the prison. Peter was free!
God answered his friends' prayers.

Paul and Silas in Jail

Acts 16:16-40

Paul and Silas were in jail.
But they were singing songs about God.
The other prisoners were surprised to hear that.

Suddenly there was an earthquake.
The jail shook. The doors came open.
Paul and Silas could have run away.

But they did not leave.
Paul kept all the other prisoners there, too.
That was the right thing to do.

The man in charge of the prisoners knew they could have run away. Now he wanted to learn about Jesus, too!

Paul Is Shipwrecked

Acts 27:9-44

Paul was a prisoner on a ship.
It was sailing for Rome.
When he got there, a king would
decide if Paul should be put to death.

But a big storm came up on the sea.
The wind blew hard against the ship.
Rain pounded down on it.

The ship crashed onto some rocks.
It broke into pieces. But Paul was
not hurt. No one was hurt!

God took care of Paul.
God still had important things
for Paul to do for Him.

Heaven

John 14:1-4; Revelation 21

Jesus is in heaven with God.
He told His followers that He was
getting a place ready for them.

Jesus promised that someday He would come back and get His followers. He would take them to heaven to be with Him.

Heaven is a wonderful place.
It is filled with God's love.
It is beautiful.
There is no sadness there.

Anyone who loves Jesus will go to heaven someday.
Jesus promised that. Do you love Jesus?
Have you asked Him into your heart?